RHODE ISLAND

Past and Present

Adam Furgang

rosen publishing's
rosen central

New York

For my mother, who tells stories of her childhood in Providence, the most memorable being when a truck going up Jenckes Street broke open and watermelons rolled down the hill for all the children to chase and eat

Published in 2011 by The Rosen Publishing Group, Inc.
29 East 21st Street, New York, NY 10010

Copyright © 2011 by The Rosen Publishing Group, Inc.

First Edition

Library of Congress Cataloging-in-Publication Data

Furgang, Adam.
Rhode Island: past and present / Adam Furgang.—1st ed.
    p. cm.—(The United States: past and present)
Includes bibliographical references and index.
ISBN 978-1-4358-9494-5 (library binding)
ISBN 978-1-4358-9521-8 (pbk. book)
ISBN 978-1-4358-9555-3 (6-pack)
1. Rhode Island—Juvenile literature. I. Title.
F79.3.F87 2011
974.5—dc22

2010001451

Manufactured in Malaysia

CPSIA Compliance Information: Batch #S10YA: For further information, contact Rosen Publishing, New York, New York, at 1-800-237-9932.

On the cover: Top left: The 1901 oil painint *The Burning of the Gaspee*, by Howard Pyle. Top right: Buildings downtown Providence. Bottom: The North Lighthouse on Block Island.

Contents

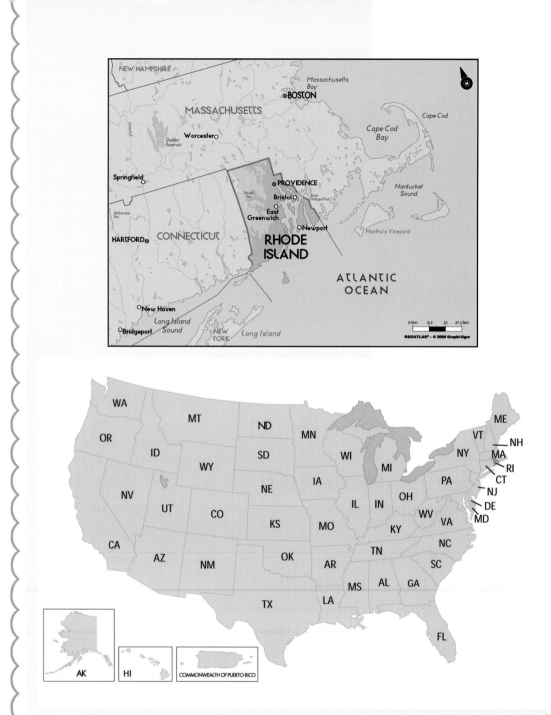

Rhode Island is located on the Atlantic Ocean. It is bordered on the west by Connecticut and to the north and east by Massachusetts. To its south lies New York State's Long Island. Rhode Island is the smallest state in the country by area, though it is also one of the most densely populated.

Introduction

Although Rhode Island is only 59 miles (95 kilometers) long and 40 miles (64 km) wide—the smallest of the fifty states—it is big on history and beauty. People can drive almost anyplace in the state in an hour or less and explore a variety of landscapes that attract visitors from around the country and the world. A trip through Rhode Island reveals coastlines, islands, ocean bay towns, forests, rivers, major cities, and small communities.

Rhode Island is one of the six northeastern states that make up the region of New England. The state is bordered on the northeast by Massachusetts and to the west by Connecticut. The rest of Rhode Island's border runs along the Atlantic Ocean. Although most of Rhode Island is part of America's mainland (and therefore not an island at all), the state does have quite a few islands off its coastline that are considered part of the state. Rhode Island's nickname is the Ocean State. Its official name is Rhode Island and the Providence Plantations, reflecting the two distinct original settlements that were joined to form the colony.

The area comprising the original Rhode Island settlement is now called Aquidneck Island and includes Newport and the towns of Portsmouth and Middletown. Historical accounts vary, but the name "Rhode Island" comes from one of two sources. Some historians claim that Dutch explorer Adriaen Block called the area *Roodt Eylandt* (meaning "Red Island," for its red clay banks along the shore).

Others say that Italian explorer Giovanni da Verrazano named it after the Isle of Rhodes in the Aegean Sea. Providence Plantations occupies the area now comprising the city of Providence, Rhode Island's state capital.

More than one million people live in Rhode Island. That is not that many people when you think about the fact that more than eight million people live in New York City. Rhode Island is famous for its beautiful mansions located in Newport, on the island of Aquidneck, as well as for its old mill buildings that once held machinery for industry. The state is home to Brown University, the Rhode Island School of Design, and many large businesses.

Rhode Island's most famous historical figure, Roger Williams, helped establish the colony several hundred years ago in a quest for religious freedom. Since then, people have settled in Rhode Island so that they can live in a place where all people are accepted and allowed to pursue their lives, religions, and beliefs in peace. With this freedom, the citizens of Rhode Island have gone on to do great things. There are many Rhode Island residents working in the areas of literature, entertainment, sports, and government.

Chapter 1

THE GEOGRAPHY OF RHODE ISLAND

Rhode Island is the country's smallest state, measuring only 1,045 square miles (2,707 square kilometers). To get an idea of just how small that is, compare it to Alaska, the largest U.S. state, with 656,425 square miles (1,700,133 sq km).

The state's geography is divided into two major regions. The first is the Coastal Lowlands, located in the southern and eastern areas of the state. The second region is the New England Upland in the northern and western areas of the state. The Coastal Lowlands are the larger of the regions, accounting for two-thirds of Rhode Island's total area. The Coastal Lowlands include most of the mainland and the islands in Narragansett Bay. Most of Rhode Island's population, as well as its major cities, is located in the Coastal Lowlands.

Salt Marshes and Narragansett Bay

There are many salt marshes in Rhode Island. A salt marsh is an area of grassland that is normally flooded by ocean water. These marshes, along with beautiful sandy beaches and shallow ponds, make up the landscape of the Coastal Lowlands.

A huge variety of wildlife lives in and around the marshes and coastal areas. Fish such as mummichogs, menhaden, and striped

The great blue heron is one of the many birds that lives among Rhode Island's marshes in the Coastal Lowlands.

bass make their home there, as do invertebrates such as quahogs, oysters, mussels, fiddler crabs, and snails. In addition, many birds come to the marshes to eat. Osprey, herons, and all sorts of ducks search for food in the marshes. There are even mosquito-eating sparrows that nest in the marsh. The salt marshes act as nature's water filters because they help reduce inland pollutants before they reach coastal waters. The salt marshes also serve as natural barriers to help protect inland areas from coastal flooding. Rocky cliffs offer spectacular views of the Narragansett Bay, and the ocean defines some of the state's unique features.

Narragansett Bay, which contains three large islands and dozens of smaller ones, extends 28 miles (45 km) inland. Aquidneck Island is the largest of the state's islands. This is where the city of Newport is located. Prudence Island and Conanicut Island are also located within Narragansett Bay. The fourth-largest island, Block Island, is located 12 miles (19 km) out in the Atlantic Ocean.

Coastal Plains and Inland Forests

Farther inland, the Coastal Lowlands begin to rise into coastal plains, some of which are used as farmland. Eventually, these plains begin to yield to forests and woods that cover more than half of the state.

Back in the nineteenth century, fewer acres of Rhode Island's land were covered by forest than today. This is because more of the state's land was used for farming, and forests have now sprung up on the abandoned farmland. Hickory, oak, pine, and maple trees are common in Rhode Island's woods and forests. It is not unusual to see old rock walls in these woodlands. These walls were built when the land was cleared for farming hundreds of years ago. They also doubled as property boundaries. They have survived despite the reversion of the farmland to forest.

Block Island is located off the south shore of Rhode Island. Today, it is a popular tourist destination and year-round home for several hundred residents.

Wildlife within the state's forests includes many mammals such as deer, wild turkey, ruffed grouse, squirrels, and coyotes. Chipmunks, beavers, foxes, hares, moles, muskrats, opossums, raccoons, and skunks roam freely in the region. Migrating birds, like

Rhode Island's Land

The land regions that make up Rhode Island were formed during the last ice age. During this period of global cooling, massive sheets of ice, sometimes 2 miles (3.2 km) thick, covered much of North America. Throughout Earth's history there have been several significant ice ages. The last one started about 2.6 million years ago and ended around 11,700 years ago. The period of time this ice age occurred in is called the Pleistocene Epoch.

During the last great ice age, glaciers formed both regions of Rhode Island: the Coastal Lowlands and the New England Upland. Throughout this period, the Laurentide Ice Sheet advanced and retreated several times. This ice had a tremendous impact on the landscape. As the glacier moved south, it carried huge amounts of rock, soil, and clay. It also carved out ridges into the landscape called moraines. The glacier pushed south and formed terminal moraines, or end moraines. The terminal moraines marked where the glacier had halted its forward expansion. They also formed Long Island, Block Island, Cape Cod, Normans Land, Martha's Vineyard, and Nantucket, all along the East Coast of the United States.

Today, it may seem like the ancient glacier and its shaping of the land have had little effect on Rhode Island. However the irregular coastline that exists in Rhode Island is a direct result of the last ice age. The retreating glacier left behind Narragansett Bay, Block Island, Aquidneck Island, Prudence Island, and Conanicut Island. All of these islands and Rhode Island's other unique coastal features continue to have a direct impact on the region's ocean culture. Rhode Island's name and nickname, the Ocean State, both refer to the effects of the glacier-influenced landscape. The state's abundant fishing, coastal wildlife variety, and maritime and tourist industries all exist today thanks to the glaciers of the last ice age.

mourning doves and woodcocks, also use these woods as their warm-weather homes.

There are no real mountain ranges in Rhode Island. As the land reaches 200 feet (61 meters) above sea level, the New England Upland region begins. The state's highest point is only 812 feet (247.5 m) above sea level, at Jerimoth Hill.

Rivers and Reservoirs

The main rivers in Rhode Island are the Blackstone River, Pawtuxet River, and Sakonnet River. The Blackstone River flows from the northeastern part of the state heading south. Its name changes along the way. It becomes the Seekonk River and, eventually, the Providence River before emptying into Narragansett Bay. The Pawtuxet River starts at the Scituate Reservoir and leads into the Providence River.

The Scituate Reservoir is the state's largest inland body of water. It was built in the 1920s and began operation in October 1926. The reservoir was created to provide drinking water for the state's capital city of Providence. A series of tunnels and pipes connect the reservoir's water supply to the surrounding region.

Climate

Temperatures in Rhode Island are typical for New England, with a January average temperature of 29 degrees Fahrenheit (-1.67 degrees Celsius) and a July average temperature of 71°F (21.67°C). Precipitation averages 44 inches (112 centimeters) a year. About half of the state's precipitation falls in the form of snow during the winter months in the New England Upland.

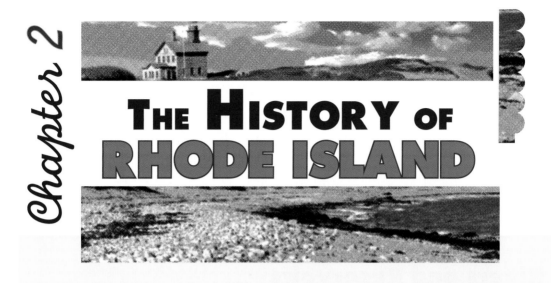

Chapter 2

THE HISTORY OF RHODE ISLAND

Not long after the last ice age ended, there were as many as ten thousand native people living in the area that is now New England. By the 1500s, their numbers had grown to around thirty thousand. These peoples made up five different tribes that lived in and around the area that is now Rhode Island. The biggest and most influential of the five tribes was the Narragansett, representing about half of the native peoples from the region. The other four tribes in the area were the Niantic, Nipmuck, Pequot, and Wampanoag.

Natives and New Arrivals

The Native American tribes of this area moved around frequently. During the summer months, they would live near the sea in wigwams made from bark and animal skins. In these summer villages, the tribes would fish, gather shellfish, and plant crops such as beans and squash. Their main crop was corn, and they planted a lot of it near their homes. During the winter months, they would move inland, where they could hunt and live in the more secure longhouses that held as many as twenty families each.

The Rhode Island region was abundant with sea life and wild game. The people who lived there thrived for many generations.

Eventually, however, many of these native peoples died off. They were killed either by diseases like smallpox, introduced by the newly arrived European explorers and settlers, or through military conflicts with the Europeans as colonization efforts increased.

It is possible that the Vikings or the Portuguese may have explored the Narragansett region prior to the sixteenth century. Yet there is no official record of European exploration in the area until 1524. This is when an Italian explorer named Giovanni da Verrazano first recorded his visit to Narragansett Bay in a diary. A Dutch sailor named Adriaen Block also explored the bay in 1614. Block Island is named after him.

The Puritans and Roger Williams

European colonization of what became known as New England began in earnest in the 1600s, when the Puritans left England to come to North America. They had hopes of practicing their own religion away from the stifling and repressive influence of the government-backed Church of England.

In 1630, Puritan minister Roger Williams left England with his wife and daughter and sailed to Massachusetts. He hoped to find religious freedom in the New World. The Puritans had escaped religious persecution in England. Yet soon after their arrival in North America, they began demanding that everyone who was part of the newly founded Massachusetts Bay Colony follow Puritan beliefs or face punishment and expulsion.

Williams was dismayed by this decision, feeling that it violated the spirit of the New World and the place of tolerance and religious freedom that they hoped to create there. His disagreements with the Massachusetts religious leaders led them to decide that he and his family should be sent back to England. Instead, Williams and his

In this picture Roger Williams meets with the Narragansett tribe, with whom he was friendly and who donated land to help found Providence Plantations.

family fled south of Boston and settled near Narragansett Bay.

Williams became friends with the native peoples in the area, and in 1636, he founded Providence on land that the Narragansett tribe gave to him. He invited people of all kinds to come and live in his new colony and practice religion any way they saw fit. He welcomed Baptists, Jews, Quakers, and even atheists—people who don't believe in a god or higher being at all.

The Puritans were deeply offended and infuriated by this. They tried to gain control of the new colony and put a stop to Williams's freethinking ways. Eventually, Williams helped convince England's King Charles II to halt the Puritans' efforts to seize the new settlement. In 1644, Charles issued a charter calling for the creation of Rhode Island and the Providence Plantations as an official colony of Great Britain that would be under the king's protection.

Rebellious Rhode Island

As with the other original thirteen American colonies, Rhode Island was both protected by the British Crown and ruled by it. Over time, the colonists came to cherish the protection less and resent the rule more. Britain was making it difficult for colonists to profit from selling their own goods. New taxes were created, and the creation of certain items, such as iron and cloth, was outlawed.

As a result of the growing fury over these repressive laws and taxes and a lack of representation in the British Parliament, revolutionary fervor began to build throughout the colonies. Rhode Island was the first to declare independence from Great Britain on May 4, 1776. The colonies were tired of being ruled by the king and decided to band together, shake off the British yoke, and govern themselves.

While Rhode Island was the first to declare independence from Britain, it was the last to approve the basic laws of the United States, known as the Constitution. This governing document was drafted and ratified following the American Revolution. Rhode Island did finally approve the Constitution on May 29, 1790, making it the thirteenth state to join the Union.

The Industrial Revolution

The very same year that Rhode Island became a state, the Industrial Revolution began to gather steam in the United States. Rhode Island was at the center of this movement toward machine power (as opposed to human or horsepower) because it was the place where the country's first water-run cotton mill was built.

An English immigrant named Samuel Slater built the machine. He did not invent the cotton mill but memorized the intricate design of an English mill that he had worked in for seven years before coming to America. Sir Richard Arkwright was the person who actually invented the useful machine that spun cotton into yarn. The

Religious Freedom

When Rhode Island was first established as a colony, the idea of religious freedom was extremely important to its settlers. They had come from countries where they were persecuted for their religious beliefs. The laws of European society were often made and enforced by the dominant church or religion because religious leaders worked in close cooperation with political and military leaders. Sometimes religious leaders were also the political and military leaders.

When people began hearing news of Rhode Island, where church and state were kept separate and religious freedom was fostered, persecuted and oppressed religious minorities began flocking there. Many of them came from Massachusetts. This colony was governed by the Puritans. Though once themselves persecuted for their beliefs, they imposed a religious government that tolerated no disagreement with its ministers or deviation from their moral principles and articles of faith. Rhode Island provided a safe haven for Baptists, Quakers, and Jews, in particular. Presbyterians and Episcopalians also found a home there.

Today, those faiths are still represented in Rhode Island. Yet the state's dominant religion is Catholicism, with Catholics making up more than 60 percent of the population. This is an interesting historical development because, despite Rhode Island's celebrated tradition of religious freedom and tolerance, very few Catholics settled there until the nineteenth century. In 1680, there were no recorded Catholic colonists, and by 1828, there were fewer than one thousand Catholics in the state. Thanks to emigration from Ireland, Portugal, Italy, and French Canada, however, their numbers swelled over time. Recent Hispanic immigration has further increased the Catholic presence in the state.

The state's status as a haven for religious minorities persists. A small percentage of the population is Muslim, and 6 percent of Rhode Island's citizens are atheists. Rhode Island is also home to a small but robust "Old Catholic" population, made up of dissenting Catholics who object to church teachings on divorce, birth control, female priests, and homosexuality.

construction and mechanics of the English cotton gin were kept a secret because Arkwright hoped to get an exclusive patent on the invention and have a monopoly over the cotton milling industry. For this reason, those who worked in his mills were not allowed to leave the country. Slater, though he knew it was illegal, eventually snuck out of England dressed as a farmer to make his fortune in North America.

Samuel Slater became known as the father of American industry, thanks to his introduction of cotton mills to the United States.

Water from Rhode Island's rivers powered Slater's mills. Dams were created so that there would be a constant supply of water available to provide energy. Eventually, Slater began using steam power to run the mills. This allowed the mills to be set up anywhere, not just near a source of running water. Soon, steam replaced water as the dominant power source for manufacturing.

Through Slater's enterprising efforts, Rhode Island became the center of the Industrial Revolution. Many textile mills were set up around the state, ultimately employing about half of the state's workers. That meant about half of Rhode Island's working residents were busy manufacturing goods. In the wake of industrialization, only 10 percent of the workforce worked on farms, and only 3 percent fished for a living in the Ocean State.

The Breakers is one of the most famous mansions in Newport. It is the foremost symbol of Rhode Island's manufacturing-driven prosperity and is now one of the state's major tourist destinations. This seventy-room home built for the Vanderbilt family is open to the public for tours.

Difficult Changes and New Opportunities

In the middle of the nineteenth century, sharp divisions between the Northern and Southern states grew as the debate over slavery became more and more important in American politics and society. The country was thrust into a civil war after the Southern states, refusing to abolish slavery, began to secede from the nation. During the Civil War, Rhode Island began to prosper because, as a highly industrialized state, it soon became a major center of wartime industry. Weapons, including cannons and rifles, were made there. The many textile mills in the state also helped produce blankets, uniforms, and tents for the Union Army.

After the war ended, manufacturing in Rhode Island continued to grow. By the early 1900s, Providence had the world's largest file factory, tool factory, screw factory, silverware factory, and steam engine factory. After the process of gold plating was invented, less-precious metals could be used to make attractive costume jewelry, which was inexpensive but looked costly. Large costume jewelry factories were established in Providence, and the city became famous for its jewelry district.

As the 1900s approached, change came to Rhode Island. Many manufacturing plants moved south in search of cheaper labor and lower state taxes. Textile manufacturing was still important, but the earlier boom days were gone for good. Then the stock market crash of 1929 dragged the entire country into the Great Depression. Millions of people lost their jobs, and the once-mighty textile industry shrank even more. By 1937, almost 80 percent of Rhode Island's cotton mills had closed.

Despite this major shift in its economy, Rhode Island continues to prosper. Manufacturing is still important but now sits alongside other important industries, such as tourism, banking, and health care. Many of the textile mills that were vacant for decades are being restored and converted into condominiums for people to live in. Many of the historical sites from Rhode Island's past are museums today. People from around the world come to visit Rhode Island to see Samuel Slater's cotton mill in Pawtucket, the mansions of Newport, and the historical buildings and neighborhoods of Providence. They are all lovingly preserved to showcase the state's heritage.

Chapter 3

THE GOVERNMENT OF RHODE ISLAND

The state government of Rhode Island operates much the same way that the federal government does. It has three parts: the executive branch, the legislative branch, and the judicial branch.

Executive Branch

The governor is in charge of Rhode Island's executive branch. Like the president of the United States, the governor is elected to a four-year term. The governor is the political head of state and has many important responsibilities. When the legislative branch passes a bill (a proposed law), it is the governor's job to accept or reject it. If the governor agrees with a bill, he or she will sign it and the bill will become a law. If the governor disagrees with a bill or thinks it needs reworking, he or she will veto (reject) it, and it will not become a law. The governor is also in charge of preparing the state budget, which tells how and where the state's money will be spent each year.

Legislative Branch

Rhode Island's legislative branch is very similar to the U.S. Congress. The state legislature consists of two parts, the senate and the house

Rhode Island's capitol building is located in Providence. The structure was completed in 1901, one year after Providence was declared the permanent capital of Rhode Island.

of representatives. The house has seventy-five representatives, and the senate has thirty-eight senators. Together, the two chambers are referred to as the general assembly. They meet in the Rhode Island State House, which is located in Providence.

Bills are introduced in the general assembly. Once senators and representatives pass a bill, it is sent on to the executive branch to either be signed and put into law or vetoed. The general assembly can still pass a law over the governor's veto if the bill gets a

A Capital City

In the early days of Rhode Island, there was not any one city that served as the state capital. Since colonial times, Rhode Island had held its general assembly meetings in different cities. They would switch between Kingston, East Greenwich, Bristol, Newport, and Providence. The general assembly did this in an effort to be fair. Legislators did not want one region to be known over others as the place of government, so they held the meetings in one town in each of Rhode Island's five counties. In 1854, the legislative sessions began to rotate between Newport and Providence. Finally, in 1900, the state constitution was amended to declare that legislative meetings would only take place in Providence, the city that had evolved from Roger Williams's original settlement founded in 1636.

Today, Providence is the state capital and permanent meeting place of the general assembly. It is also where the office of the governor and lieutenant governor is located.

Providence went through a period of decline when manufacturing moved away from the city and many mills closed down. Starting in the 1970s, however, the city began to be rebuilt and revitalized. Hundreds of millions of dollars went into improving the capital. Years before, the city's natural rivers had been paved over. As part of urban renewal efforts, Providence's rivers were again uncovered and made available for public use. A new convention center, skating rink, urban park, and riverwalk were created to attract visitors.

The plan worked. Providence became a major center of tourism and began to reverse a trend of population loss that had begun as early as the 1920s. Today, the city is a modern metropolis with high-rise office and apartment towers, hotels, leading hospitals, and nationally recognized colleges, universities, and cultural institutions. These include Brown University and the Rhode Island School of Design.

three-fifths majority of votes in favor of it. This way, the governor cannot wield too much power over the other branches of government. It is also the job of the legislative branch to approve or reject the proposed budget that is sent to the general assembly from the governor's office each year.

Judicial Branch

The third branch of Rhode Island's government is the judicial branch. The highest judicial court is the state supreme court, which is made up of five judges who are appointed for life (or until voluntary retirement). Since 1994, the governor of Rhode Island has been appointing these justices. Before that time, the legislative branch had appointed the judges. After the governor makes an appointment, both houses of the legislative branch must approve the choice.

The Rhode Island Superior Court building in Providence is where the state supreme court judges meet and work.

Chapter 4

THE ECONOMY OF RHODE ISLAND

Rhode Island's economy has changed a lot throughout its history. From the time of the first European settlements, the sea has been an important resource for the local economy. Fishing and farming were the main sources of income for many of the state's residents. The ocean provided more lobster and salmon than people knew what to do with. While fishing is still part of the economy today, it is no longer the chief way of earning a living in the state.

Triangular Trade

During the 1700s, some of Rhode Island's wealthiest colonists became involved in the extremely profitable trade of rum, molasses, sugar, money, and slaves that became known as the triangular trade. The trade involved three regions and three types of cargo. In Rhode Island, kegs of rum were loaded onto merchant ships. From there, the rum was shipped to and sold in West Africa, where it was traded for African slaves. Some of the Africans were shipped to the West Indies to be traded for molasses, money, and sugar. The cargo of molasses and sugar then returned to Rhode Island to be distilled into more rum. Any remaining slaves onboard were sold to Rhode Island colonists.

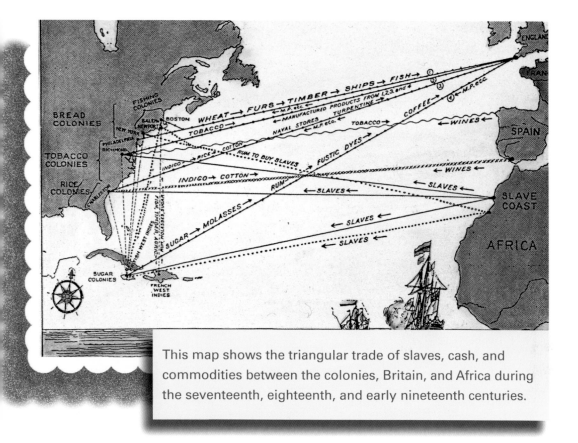

This map shows the triangular trade of slaves, cash, and commodities between the colonies, Britain, and Africa during the seventeenth, eighteenth, and early nineteenth centuries.

Much like in the southern colonies, the use of slaves in the North helped create profits for merchants. As a result, wealth grew in Rhode Island. The sale of slaves did not last forever, though. Rhode Island outlawed it in 1774, long before other colonies in the North. Some of the wooden houses that slaves built at the time are still standing in Newport today.

Manufacturing

The construction of Samuel Slater's textile mills was an important turning point not only for Rhode Island's economy, but also for the

Workers on a treadmill provided the power to
Samuel Slater's first cotton mill in Pawtucket.

entire United States. Slater became known as the father of the
American Industrial Revolution. From the late 1700s and early 1800s,
the mills made Rhode Island an important place for people to find
employment. Working in textile factories paid more, and the income
was more reliable than farming and fishing. Cotton mills became
bigger, and they employed more and more people. One cotton mill
in Providence became known as the biggest in the world. Mills in

Rhode Island manufactured many of the uniforms used in the Civil War.

Once factories became commonplace, the cotton mill was no longer the only choice for workers. Rhode Island opened factories to make metal products, including tools, hardware, and cutlery. By 1900, Providence boasted the largest tool factory (Brown & Sharpe), file factory (Nicholson File), engine factory (Corliss Steam Engine Company),

This U.S. Navy ship is being loaded with equipment and cargo at Newport. Newport is home to Naval Station Newport and the Naval War College.

screw factory (American Screw), and silverware factory (Gorham) in the world. At this time, there were 144 machine shops in Rhode Island, employing nearly 8,800 workers.

However, just as the farming and fishing industries changed over time, so, too, did manufacturing. Many factories and mills moved to the southern states where taxes, land, and salaries were cheaper. As a result, Rhode Island was forced to adapt to changing circumstances and new opportunities in the twentieth century.

Economic Diversification

As the twentieth century got under way, the most important industries in Rhode Island remained textiles, metals, and machinery. Yet jewelry and silverware also became very important to the state's

Rhode Island Tourism

In colonial times, most families did not go on vacation and take time off to visit new places. Many had no break from their farming or merchant responsibilities and little, if any, money to spend on leisure. Only the wealthiest people visited faraway places. In fact, the word "tourism" was not coined until 1811. When the wealthy traveled in the late 1800s or early 1900s, they tended to visit Europe to see the Old World's treasures of art and architecture. There were few attractions in Rhode Island that would draw people from other states, let alone other countries.

Today, tourism is the backbone of Rhode Island's economy. Among the most modern and popular tourist attractions in Rhode Island are the WaterFire events in Providence. A sculpture that floats on the city's three rivers is the centerpiece of a tourist event that occurs every weekend night from March to October. One hundred bonfires are lit on the floating sculpture, and torch-lit boats sail along the rivers past the festivities that include music, food, and entertainment. Since starting in 1994, the event has attracted more than ten million visitors to the city, with an average of 350,000 per year. More than 60 percent of the visitors to WaterFire are from outside Rhode Island.

When tourists are attracted to a particular locality, they bring money into the area by eating in restaurants, staying in hotels, and buying goods in local shops. Tourism is an important industry in many states, and people who visit Rhode Island tend to visit more than one city. Newport, the Newport Jazz Festival, the Newport Folk Festival, Narragansett, Block Island, and the beaches of Westerly are also international tourist attractions. Tourism accounts for more than $3 billion in annual revenue for the state.

economy. During World War II, Rhode Island began making electrical equipment, plastic, and rubber items. The U.S. Navy and its facilities in Newport provided a lot of work for people and kept the economy going.

Today, tourism has become one of the state's most important sources of income, second only to health care services. Among the most popular tourist attractions in the state are the Newport mansions. People visit the many grand houses of Newport and marvel at the architecture and beautiful ocean views while taking a 3.5-mile (5.6 km) cliff walk around the shoreline.

The mansions are the pride of Newport. Many of the grand houses were built during the late 1800s by wealthy families who made their money during the Industrial Revolution. One of the most famous mansions, The Breakers, was built as a summer home by Cornelius Vanderbilt II. The seventy-room home is situated on 13 acres (5 hectares) of beautiful gardens. It is the most visited attraction in the state and brings more than three hundred thousand people to Newport each year.

Chapter 5

PEOPLE FROM RHODE ISLAND:
PAST AND PRESENT

Roger Williams and Samuel Slater are not the only people who have helped shape the history of Rhode Island. The state is home to many people who have had a big influence on the state, the country, and even the world. Rhode Island residents have made great contributions in art, cinema, music, literature, journalism, politics, and the military.

Everett Arnold (1899–1974) Everett Arnold, born in Providence, grew up to be an entrepreneur in the comic book industry. The 1930s and 1940s were known as the Golden Age of Comics. Arnold was the publisher of Quality Comics, a company whose stable of characters included the Spirit, Wildfire, Choo-Choo, Spider Widow, and Manhunter.

Wendy Carlos (1939–) Wendy Carlos, born in Pawtucket, is a pioneer of electronic music. Beginning in the 1960s, she was the first musician to demonstrate that the synthesizer could be used as a legitimate instrument, rather than a mere novelty machine that made wacky noises. Using Robert Moog's revolutionary synthesizer, Carlos created electronic versions of classical compositions, most famously Bach selections. Her soundtracks for movies like *A Clockwork Orange*, *The Shining*, and *Tron* further revealed how versatile and beautiful synthesized music could be. Her work laid the foundation for much of the electronic and ambient music that would later gain mainstream acceptance.

Thomas W. Dorr (1805–1854) Thomas W. Dorr was born in Providence. He was very involved in politics and played a major role in Dorr's Rebellion in 1842. Dorr and his fellow rebels sought voting reform that would extend the right to vote beyond only those Rhode Islanders who

Thomas Dorr was sentenced to solitary confinement and hard labor for life by the Rhode Island Supreme Court for his role in the rebellion that bore his name.

owned land or property. At this time, Rhode Island was one of the only states that had not granted the right to vote to all adult white males.

Peter Farrelly (1956–) and Bobby Farrelly (1958–) Peter and Bobby Farrelly are filmmakers who are known professionally as the Farrelly brothers. Bobby was born in Cumberland, and both grew up in that town. Their most popular films include *Dumb and Dumber*, *Kingpin*, and *There's*

The People of Rhode Island

The size and density of Rhode Island's population has changed greatly over time. From the days of its first colonial charter with England, Rhode Island was a small settlement mainly made up of farmers and fishermen. Into the nineteenth century, Rhode Island remained a small settlement. At the time of the adoption of the Constitution in 1787, it is estimated that only fifty-eight thousand to sixty-five thousand people were living in Rhode Island. In comparison, Massachusetts and Pennsylvania had more than 350,000 residents, and Virginia's population was greater than 400,000.

It was the Industrial Revolution that dramatically changed the population of Rhode Island. Suddenly, cities began to develop where rural areas once were. As factories were built, city populations grew. People left farms and moved to cities for more secure jobs.

Today, although Rhode Island remains the smallest state in the country, it is the second most densely populated. There are about a thousand people living in each square mile (2.6 sq km) of the state. The national average is seventy-nine people per square mile. Roughly 1,050,000 people live in Rhode Island. Ninety percent of Rhode Island's more than one million residents live in cities. The population is most concentrated in Providence County and in the former mill towns. The state's largest ancestry groups include the Irish, Italians, Portuguese, French Canadians, English, and Hispanics (mostly Puerto Rican and Dominican). African immigrants are a significant and growing population. Many of them come from Ghana, Liberia, Cape Verde, and Nigeria. Eleven percent of Rhode Islanders are foreign born. Most of them have emigrated from Europe and Latin America. Twenty percent of Rhode Island households converse in a language other than English. More than 60 percent of the state's residents were born and raised in Rhode Island.

Something About Mary. They have also worked on an updating of the Three Stooges characters. In 1999, they wrote the screenplay for *Outside Providence*. This is an autobiographical tale of a troubled blue-collar Pawtucket teen who is sent to an elite prep school, where he struggles with richer but no less troubled classmates.

Nathanael Greene (1742–1786)

Continental Army officer Nathanael Greene of Warwick entered the Continental Army at the

General Nathanael Greene of Warwick helped lead the Continental Army during the American Revolution. He rose to become commander of all the Southern forces.

lowest rank. By the time the American Revolution was over, however, he was one of the biggest heroes of the war. He was personal friends with George Washington and took responsibility for especially difficult military challenges. These included the Battle of Lexington and Concord in Boston and the defense of New York City against British attacks. Eventually, Washington appointed him quartermaster-general.

H. P. Lovecraft (1890–1937) Born in Providence, H. P. Lovecraft is one of the most influential horror and science fiction writers of the twentieth century. He did not have a large readership while he was alive because fantasy and science fiction were not yet well known or understood by many people. In fact, horror, fantasy, and science fiction were then known as weird fiction. Lovecraft now has a cult following and has inspired many other writers. There have been movies, TV programs, games, music, art, and comics based on his works. He died in the same town where he was born.

Pulitzer Prize–winning author Cormac McCarthy was born in Providence. He is considered one of America's greatest living novelists.

Cormac McCarthy (1933–) The author Cormac McCarthy was born in Providence. He won the Pulitzer Prize in 2007 for his novel *The Road*. His other works include *All the Pretty Horses* and *No Country for Old Men*. *No Country for Old Men* was made into an Academy Award–winning film by the directors Joel and Ethan Coen in 2007.

This artwork depicts artist Gilbert Stuart painting a portrait of George Washington. It is an engraving based on this Stuart portrait that would eventually appear on the $1 bill. The portrait was begun by Stuart in 1796 but remained unfinished at his death in 1828.

Walter Mossberg (1947–) Newspaper columnist Walter Mossberg was born in Warwick. He is a well-known writer and editor for the *Wall Street Journal*, where he has worked since 1970. In recent years, he has turned from national and international affairs to technology issues. He is one of the nation's leading authorities on information technology. In 2001, he won the World Technology Award for Media and Journalism and received an honorary doctorate of law from the University of Rhode Island.

Gilbert Stuart (1755–1828) Painter Gilbert Stuart was born in Saunderstown. He was a famous portrait painter and is best known for a portrait of George Washington that he finished in 1796. A copy of that image appeared on the $1 bill for more than a hundred years.

Mena Suvari (1979–) Mena Suvari was born in Newport and is an actress best known for her roles in the films *American Beauty* and *American Pie*. She is also an active campaigner for women's issues, especially the fights against breast cancer and violence against women.

Timeline

1636	Providence is founded by Roger Williams.
1663	King Charles II grants the Charter of Rhode Island and Providence Plantations on July 8. This charter serves as Rhode Island's constitution until 1842.
1772	British trade restrictions anger Rhode Island's colonists. Protests grow throughout the colony.
1776	The colony declares its independence from Great Britain on May 4.
1776–1779	British forces occupy Newport.
1784	The Emancipation Act passes in the general assembly, providing for the gradual abolition of slavery in Rhode Island. All African American children born after March 1, 1784, are considered free.
1790	Rhode Island is granted statehood on May 29.
1793	The first successful American cotton mill is established by Samuel Slater and David Wilkinson in Pawtucket.
1842	Dorr's Rebellion forces the charter of 1663 to be abandoned, and voting rights are expanded.
1843	Rhode Island's present state constitution is adopted.
1847	The first train runs through Rhode Island.
1895	The Breakers, Cornelius Vanderbilt's Newport mansion, is completed.
1936	Rhode Island celebrates its three hundredth anniversary.
1980	Claudine Schneider is the first woman elected to Congress from Rhode Island.
1994	WaterFire celebrations start on Providence's rivers.
2009	Claiborne Pell, a six-term Rhode Island senator and the driving force behind Pell college grants, dies on January 1.
2010	Rhode Island congressional representative Patrick J. Kennedy announces he will not run for reelection, marking the end of an era and a political dynasty. This is the first time a Kennedy has not served in Congress since 1947.

State motto:	"Hope"
State capital:	Providence
State tree:	Red maple
State bird:	Rhode Island red hen
State flower:	Violet
State stone:	Cumberlandite
Statehood date and number:	May 29, 1790; thirteenth state
State nickname:	The Ocean State
Total area and U.S. rank:	1,045 square miles (2,707 sq km); fiftieth largest state
Population:	1,050,788
Length of coastline:	More than 400 miles (644 km)
Highest elevation:	Jerimoth Hill, at 812 feet (247.5 m)
Lowest elevation:	Sea level, where the coast meets the Atlantic Ocean, at 0 feet (0 m)

State Flag

State Seal

Major rivers:	Blackstone River, Branch River, Pawcatuck River, Pawtuxet River, Ponaganset River, Providence River, Sakonnet River, Usquepaug River, Wood River, Woonasquatucket River
Major lakes:	Flat River Reservoir, Pascoag Lake, Scituate Reservoir, Smith and Sayles Reservoir, Worden Pond
Highest recorded temperature:	104°F (40°C) in Providence, August 2, 1975
Lowest recorded temperature:	-25°F (-32°C) in Greene, February 6, 1996
Origin of state name:	Possibly named after the Greek Island of Rhodes or derived from the Dutch *Roodt Eylandt* ("Red Island")
Chief agricultural products:	Sod, trees, shrubs, corn, apples, milk
Major industries:	Electrical equipment, costume jewelry, silverware

Rhode Island red hen

Violet

GLOSSARY

bill A proposed law subject to a legislature's vote for passage or rejection and an executive's signing or veto.

charter Written permission that grants power to a group.

economy The way that the people of an area use their resources and environment to meet their needs and make money.

executive branch The branch of government that signs and carries out laws, led by a president, governor, or similar leader.

glacier A slow-moving mass of ice.

judicial branch The branch of government that enforces laws and judges their fairness, justness, or constitutionality. This branch includes the court system.

legislative branch The branch of government that makes laws.

manufacturing The business of making goods on a large scale using machinery.

mill A building that holds machinery for industry; a factory.

moraine A mass of rocks deposited by a glacier.

persecuted Treated badly or harshly, usually for one's beliefs or racial or ethnic background.

prosper To succeed, grow, develop, and become wealthy.

Puritans An English Protestant religious group of the sixteenth, seventeenth, and eighteenth centuries, characterized by their strict morality and a reliance on biblical guidance for all aspects of life, including government.

salt marsh An area of grassland that is normally flooded by ocean water.

textile A type of material that is woven into fabric.

tourist A person visiting a place for pleasure.

veto To reject.

Junior Achievement of Rhode Island

270 Weybosset Street

Providence, RI 02903

(401) 331-3850

Web site: http://www.ri.ja.org

Junior Achievement of Rhode Island is an organization that provides educational programs for youth interested in business economics.

Newport Historical Society

82 Touro Street

Newport, RI 02840

(401) 846-0813

Web site: http://www.newporthistorical.org

The Newport Historical Society collects and preserves artifacts, photographs, documents, publications, and genealogical records that relate to the history of Newport County. It makes these materials readily available for both research and enjoyment.

Office of the Governor

State House, Room 115

Providence, RI 02903

(401) 222-2080

Web site: http://www.governor.ri.gov

The official Web site of the governor of Rhode Island offers news, information, events listings, accomplishments, video clips, veto messages, and new initiatives.

Preservation Society of Newport County

424 Bellevue Avenue

Newport, RI 02840

(401) 847-1000

Web site: http://www.newportmansions.org

The Preservation Society of Newport County is a nonprofit organization whose mission is to protect, preserve, and present an exceptional collection of house museums and landscapes in one of the most historically intact cities in America.

Providence CityArts for Youth

891 Broad Street

P.O. Box 27691

Providence, RI 02907

(401) 228-3718

Web site: http://www.providencecityarts.org

Providence CityArts for Youth is a nonprofit community organization that provides free art education and training for the youth of Providence.

Providence Department of Art, Culture, and Tourism

City Hall, Room 111

25 Dorrance Street

Providence, RI 02903

(401) 421-2489

Web site: http://www.providenceri.com/ArtCultureTourism

The Providence Department of Art, Culture, and Tourism ensures the continued development of a vibrant and creative city by integrating arts and culture into community life while showcasing Providence as an international cultural destination.

Rhode Island School of Design Museum of Art

224 Benefit Street

Providence, RI 02903

(401) 454-6500

Web site: http://www.risdmuseum.org

Also known as the RISD Museum, this institution is Rhode Island's leading museum of fine and decorative art. It houses a collection of eighty-four thousand objects of international significance.

Rhode Island Tourism Division

315 Iron Horse Way, Suite 101

Providence, RI 02908

(800) 250-7384

Web site: http://www.visitrhodeisland.com

This is the official Web site of the Rhode Island Tourism Division.

Volunteer Center of Rhode Island

655 Broad Street

Providence, RI 02907

(401) 331-2298

Web site: http://www.vcri.org

Volunteer Center of Rhode Island is an organization with hundreds of volunteer opportunities for people who want to help serve the state of Rhode Island.

Web Sites

Due to the nature of Internet links, Rosen Publishing has developed an online list of Web sites related to the subject of this book. This site is updated regularly. Please use this link to access the list:

http://www.rosenlinks.com/uspp/ripp

FOR FURTHER READING

Burgan, Michael. *Rhode Island*. New York, NY: Children's Press, 2009.

Burgan, Michael. *Roger Williams: Founder of Rhode Island*. Mankato, MN: Compass Point Books, 2006.

Deady, Kathleen W. *The Rhode Island Colony*. Mankato, MN: Coughlan Publishing, 2006.

Doherty, Craig A., and Katherine M. Doherty. *Rhode Island*. New York, NY: Facts on File, 2005.

Hallinan, Val. *Rhode Island*. Danbury, CT: Children's Press, 2008.

Jenson, Niels R. *Rhode Island*. Edina, MN: ABDO Publishing, 2009.

LaBella, Susan. *Rhode Island*. Danbury, CT: Children's Press, 2007.

Marsh, Carole. *Rhode Island Native Americans: A Kid's Look at Our State's Chiefs, Tribes, Reservations, Powwows, Lore, and More from the Past to the Present*. Peachtree City, GA: Gallopade International, 2004.

McDermott, Jesse. *Rhode Island 1636–1776* (Voices of Colonial America). Washington, DC: National Geographic Society, 2006.

Migliaccio, Fran. *Ghosts of Block Island*. Block Island, RI: Frances Huggard Migliaccio, 2005.

Migliaccio, Fran. *More Ghosts of Block Island*. Block Island, RI: Frances Huggard Migliaccio, 2009.

Miller, Jake. *The Colony of Rhode Island: A Primary Source History*. New York, NY: PowerKids Press, 2006.

Philbrick, Nathaniel. *The Mayflower and the Pilgrims' New World*. New York, NY: Puffin, 2009.

Severin, Carol. *Rhode Island*. Strongville, OH: Gareth Stevens Publishing, 2006.

BIBLIOGRAPHY

AC Comics. "Golden Age: Quality Comics." Retrieved October 2009 (http://www.accomics.com/accomics/goldenage/qualitycomics.html).

Axelrod-Contrada, Joan. *A Primary Source History of the Colony of Rhode Island.* New York, NY: Rosen Publishing Group, 2006.

Cumberlandite.com. "History of Cumberlandite." Retrieved September 2009 (http://www.cumberlandite.com/cumberlandite1_012.htm).

EastGreenwichRI.com. "About East Greenwich." Retrieved October 2009 (http://www.eastgreenwichri.com/matriarch/MultiPiecePage.asp?PageID=42&PageName=ResidentsAboutEG).

Fradin, Dennis B. *The Rhode Island Colony.* Danbury, CT: Children's Press, 1989.

Friedman, Juliet. "A History of Costume Jewelry Design in America." GuyotBrothers.com. Retrieved September 2009 (http://www.guyotbrothers.com/jewelry-history/american-costume-jewelry.htm).

Harper, Douglas. "Tourism." Online Etymology Dictionary, 2001. Retrieved October 2009 (http://www.etymonline.com/index.php?l=t&p=16).

Heathcote, Charles William. "Who Served Here? General Nathanael Greene." USHistory.org, 2006. Retrieved October 2009 (http://www.ushistory.org/valleyforge/served/greene.html).

HPLovecraft.com. "The H. P. Lovecraft Archive." Retrieved October 2009 (http://www.hplovecraft.com).

HuntFor.com. "Gilbert Stuart: 1755–1828." Retrieved October 2009 (http://www.huntfor.com/absoluteig/stuart.htm).

Klein, Ted. *Celebrate the State: Rhode Island.* New York, NY: Benchmark Books, 1999.

LawJRank.org. "Thomas Wilson Dorr." Retrieved October 2009 (http://law.jrank.org/pages/6260/Dorr-Thomas-Wilson.html).

McLoughlin, William G. *Rhode Island: A History.* New York, NY: W. W. Norton, 1986.

Rhode Island Habitat Restoration. "Rhode Island's Coastal Habitats." University of Rhode Island. Retrieved September 2009 (http://www.edc.uri.edu/restoration/html/intro/salt.htm).

State of Rhode Island General Assembly. "The Gilded Age, 1866–1899." Retrieved September 2009 (http://www.rilin.state.ri.us/studteaguide/rhodeislandhistory/chapt6.html).

State of Rhode Island General Assembly. "State of Rhode Island Senate." Retrieved September 2009 (http://www.rilin.state.ri.us).

State of Rhode Island Office of the Secretary of State. "History of Rhode Island."
    Retrieved October 2009 (http://sos.ri.gov/library/history).

Sullivan, Walter. "Great Climate Cycles Seen in Last Ice Age." *New York Times*,
    February 1, 1994. Retrieved September 2009 (http://www.nytimes.
    com/1994/02/01/science/great-climate-cycles-seen-in-last-ice-age.
    html?scp = 1&sq = %20%20%09%20Great%20Climate%20Cycles%20Seen
    %20in%20Last%20Ice%20Age&st = cse).

U.S. Census Bureau. "State and Country Quick Facts: Rhode Island." November 17, 2009.
    Retrieved December 2009 (http://quickfacts.census.gov/qfd/states/44000.html).

Warner, J. F. *Rhode Island* (Hello, U.S.A.). Minneapolis, MN: Lerner Publications, 2003.

WaterFire.org. "WaterFire Providence." Retrieved October 2009 (http://www.waterfire.
    org/about-waterfire/welcome).

INDEX

About the Author

Adam Furgang is the author of several books for the Rosen Publishing Group. He lives in upstate New York with his wife and two sons. They visit Rhode Island frequently to see his parents.

Photo Credits

Cover (top left), p. 1 (left) Wikipedia (http://en.wikipedia.org/wiki/File:Gaspee_Affair. jpg); cover (top right), p. 1 (right) Panoramic Images/Getty Images; cover (bottom) Michael Melford/Getty Images; pp. 3, 7, 12, 20, 24, 30, 37 © Shutterstock; p. 4 © GeoAtlas; p. 8 © www.istockphoto.com/Thomas Shortell; p. 9 © www.istockphoto.com/ Ed Halley; p. 14 © North Wind/North Wind Picture Archives; p. 17 SSPL/Getty Images; p. 18 Travel Ink/Getty Images; p. 21 © www.istockphoto.com/Kenneth C. Zirkel; p. 23 © Courtesy of the Rhode Island Judiciary; pp. 25, 26 © The Granger Collection; p. 27 Matt York/AFP/Getty Images; p. 31 Library of Congress Prints and Photographs Division; p. 33 MPI/Getty Images; p. 34 Jim Spellman/Getty Images; p. 35 Three Lions/Getty Images; p. 38 (left) Courtesy of Robesus, Inc.; p. 39 (left) © www.istockphoto.com/Jory Shepherd; p. 39 (right) © www.istockphoto.com/Constance McGuire.

Designer: Les Kanturek; Photo Researcher: Marty Levick